OUT OF THIS WORLD

Meet NASA Inventor Bruce Wiegmann and His Team's

Solar-Wind-Riding Electric Sail

www.worldbook.com

World Book, Inc.
180 North LaSalle Street
Suite 900
Chicago, Illinois 60601
USA

For information about other World Book publications, visit our website at www.worldbook.com or call 1-800-WORLDBK (967-5325).

For information about sales to schools and libraries, call 1-800-975-3250 (United States), or 1-800-837-5365 (Canada).

Library of Congress Cataloging-in-Publication Data for this volume has been applied for.

Out of This World
978-0-7166-6155-9 (set, hc.)

Solar-Wind-Riding Electric Sail
ISBN: 978-0-7166-6162-7 (hc.)
ISBN: 978-0-7166-6138-2 (pf.)

Also available as:
ISBN: 978-0-7166-6171-9 (e-book)

Writer: Jeff De La Rosa

Executive Committee

President
Jim O'Rourke

Vice President and
Editor in Chief
Paul A. Kobasa

Vice President, Finance
Donald D. Keller

Vice President, Marketing
Jean Lin

Vice President, International Sales
Maksim Rutenberg

Director, Human Resources
Bev Ecker

Editorial

Director, Print Content
Development
Tom Evans

Editor, Print Content Development
Kendra Muntz

Managing Editor, Science
Jeff De La Rosa

Editor, Science
William D. Adams

Librarian
S. Thomas Richardson

Manager, Contracts & Compliance
(Rights & Permissions)
Loranne K. Shields

Manager, Indexing Services
David Pofelski

Administrative Assistant, Digital
and Print Content Development
Ethel Matthews

Digital

Director, Digital Content
Development
Emily Kline

Director, Digital Product
Development
Erika Meller

Manager, Digital Products
Jonathan Wills

Graphics and Design

Senior Art Director
Tom Evans

Senior Visual Communications
Designer
Melanie Bender

Media Researcher
Rosalia Bledsoe

**Manufacturing/
Production**

Manufacturing Manager
Anne Fritzinger

Proofreader
Nathalie Strassheim

Contents

Glossary There is a glossary of terms on page 45. Terms defined in the glossary are in boldface type that **looks like this** on their first appearance on any spread (two facing pages).

Pronunciations (how to say words) are given in parentheses the first time some difficult words appear in the book. They look like this: pronunciation (pruh NUHN see AY shuhn).

Introduction

It is a long journey to the edge of the **solar system.** New Horizons was one of the fastest spacecraft ever built. It was launched in 2006 using traditional chemical rockets. First, rockets boosted the craft into orbit (a looping path) around Earth. Then, another rocket fired to speed the spacecraft toward the outer solar system. Along the way, New Horizons swung by the giant planet Jupiter. As it did, it used the planet's strong gravitational pull to slingshot itself to even greater speeds.

The solar system contains millions of objects, but most would take many years to reach with conventional rocket technology.

With all that, it still took New Horizons nearly 10 years to fly by the dwarf planet Pluto. Yet the outermost boundary of the solar system, called the **heliopause,** lies between two and three times as far away. If scientists want to truly explore the solar system's edges, they are going to need a faster way to get there.

One problem with traditional rockets is that they require a lot of fuel, in the form of chemicals called **propellants.** Propellants are heavy, usually making up most of the **mass** of the spacecraft. So while propellants help accelerate, or speed, the craft on its way, all that extra mass makes the craft more difficult to accelerate.

Engineer Bruce Wiegmann thinks he may have a solution to the propellant problem. He is working to design a new kind of spacecraft that has something in common with a sailing ship. In the past, sailing ships explored the boundaries of Earth without the use of fuel. They did so by harnessing the power of moving air—the wind.

There is no air in space. But there is an invisible flow of electrically charged particles from the sun, called the solar wind. Wiegmann's craft would ride the solar wind somewhat like a sailing ship is pushed over the seas by Earth's winds. But rather than traditional sails, the craft would fan out electrified wires around itself. The wires would *deflect* (turn away) solar wind particles. Deflecting the charged particles would push the wires away from the sun, driving Wiegmann's *electric sail* craft forward to the edges of the solar system in record time.

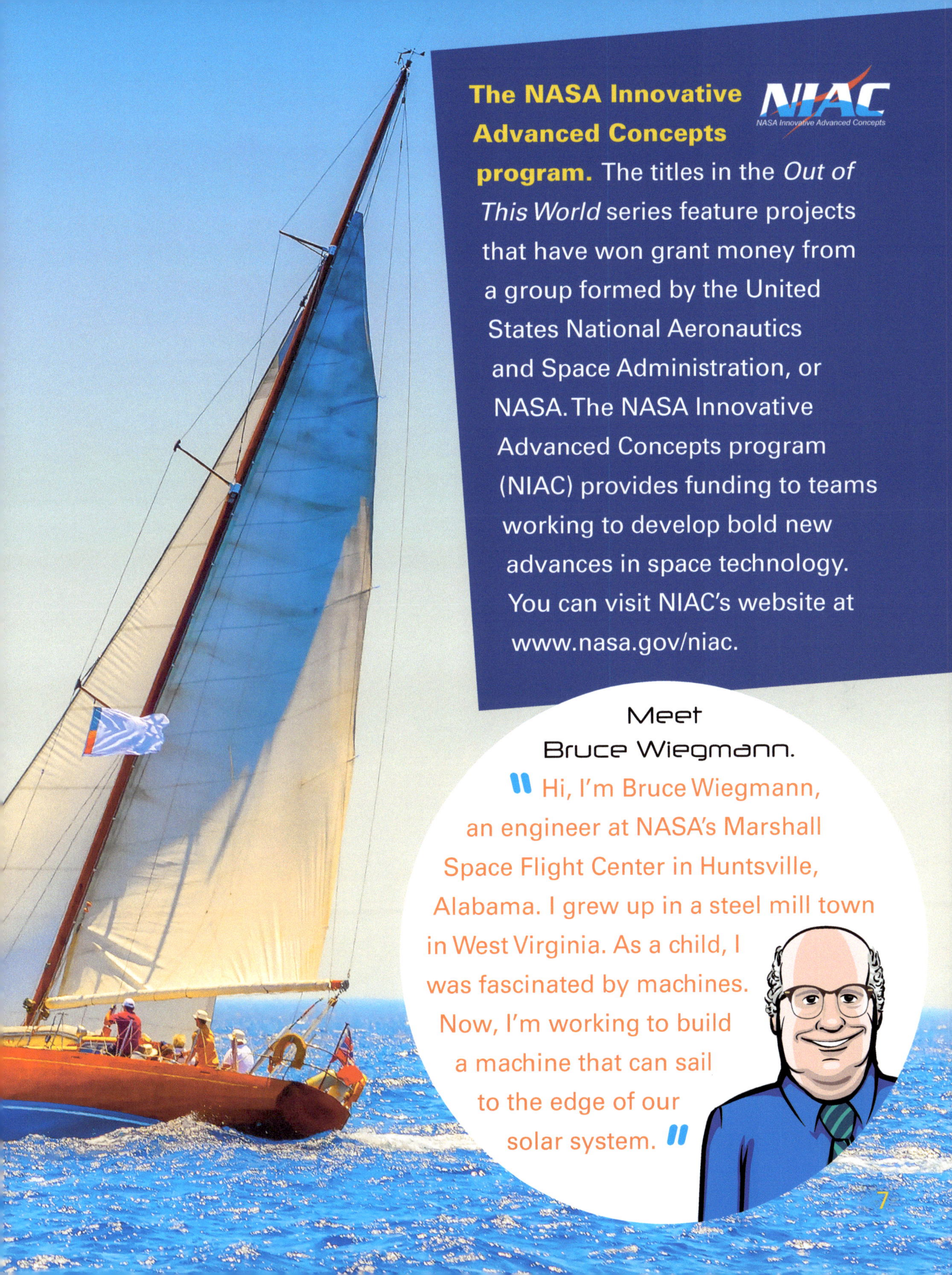

The NASA Innovative Advanced Concepts program. The titles in the *Out of This World* series feature projects that have won grant money from a group formed by the United States National Aeronautics and Space Administration, or NASA. The NASA Innovative Advanced Concepts program (NIAC) provides funding to teams working to develop bold new advances in space technology. You can visit NIAC's website at www.nasa.gov/niac.

Meet Bruce Wiegmann.

"Hi, I'm Bruce Wiegmann, an engineer at NASA's Marshall Space Flight Center in Huntsville, Alabama. I grew up in a steel mill town in West Virginia. As a child, I was fascinated by machines. Now, I'm working to build a machine that can sail to the edge of our solar system."

The solar wind

Outer space is often described as an airless, empty void—a vacuum. But the truth is that space is only mostly empty. Even the emptiest regions of space contain a few *subatomic particles* (particles smaller than atoms). In our **solar system,** most of them are electrically charged particles streaming from the sun.

These particles originate in the *corona*, the outermost layer of the sun's atmosphere. Temperatures in the corona average about 4 million degrees Fahrenheit (2.2 million degrees Celsius). Extreme heat within the corona can tear atoms apart, sending subatomic particles flying off in all directions. This flow of particles from the sun is called the solar wind.

The particles of the solar wind leave the sun at a mind-blowing speed. As they pass Earth, they are traveling about 155 to 625 miles (250 to 1,000 kilometers) per second. The particles spread out as they travel, becoming less *dense* (tightly packed) with distance. By the time the solar wind reaches Earth, it has a density equivalent to about 82 atoms per cubic inch (5 atoms per cubic centimeter). For comparison, a cubic centimeter of air near Earth's surface contains **quintillions** of atoms.

Earth's shield

Activity within Earth's core generates an invisible area of magnetic influence around the planet, called a **magnetic field.** Earth's magnetic field interacts with the charged particles of the solar wind, *diverting* (detouring) them around the planet. In this way, the magnetic field acts like a shield against the solar wind, protecting Earth's surface from dangerous radiation, a type of energy that the solar wind produces.

The edge of the solar system

The **solar wind** is a major feature of the solar system. In fact, scientists use the solar wind to determine the solar system's boundaries.

The solar wind blows throughout a roughly ball-shaped region of space known as the **heliosphere.** The sun and all the planets are inside the heliosphere. The nearest edge of the heliosphere lies about 9 billion to 15 billion miles (15 billion to 24 billion kilometers) from the sun. This distance is two to three times the distance from the sun to Pluto at the farthest point in Pluto's orbit.

Beyond the heliosphere lies interstellar space, the vast distances of space between the stars. Interstellar space is filled with a scattered mixture of particles called the interstellar medium.

As the particles of the solar wind approach the edge of the heliosphere, they begin to meet up and interact, or mix, with the interstellar medium. These interactions cause the particles of the solar wind to slow. The solar wind finally comes to a stop at a boundary called the **heliopause.** The heliopause marks the outermost edge of the solar system.

Changes in the heliosphere

From time to time, areas on the surface of the sun erupt, or blow up, into storms, flares, and other activity. Such solar activity can alter, or change, the strength of the solar wind. These alterations cause the **heliosphere** to change in size.

Think of the heliosphere as a sort of bubble in the **interstellar medium,** created by the outward push of the solar wind. In times of much solar activity, the solar wind can blow stronger. The stronger wind pushes back against the interstellar medium, moving the **heliopause** farther away. In times of little solar activity, the solar wind can weaken. This weakening causes the heliosphere to shrink, bringing the heliopause closer.

The shape of the heliosphere. The distance to the heliopause is not the same in all directions. This is because the sun and the rest of the solar system are not just standing still in the interstellar medium. Rather, the solar system appears to be moving through a cloud within the interstellar medium. The motion squeezes the heliosphere into a teardrop shape. In the direction of travel, the interstellar medium pushes the heliopause into a blunt "nose." Opposite the nose, the heliosphere stretches out into a long "tail."

Reaching the heliopause

Voyager 1, launched in 1977, took 35 years to reach the edge of the solar system.

No craft has ever been purposefully launched to explore the outermost reaches of the **heliosphere.** But spacecraft have visited the region.

In 1977, the United States launched two spacecraft to explore the outer planets of our **solar system.** The craft, called Voyager 1 and Voyager 2, revolutionized our knowledge of these planets and their satellites, whizzing by Jupiter, Saturn, Uranus, and Neptune. Voyager 1 had its last meeting with an outer planet—Saturn—in 1980. Voyager 2 had its last meeting, with Neptune, in 1989. Both craft were going too fast to stop. Instead, they continued flying off toward interstellar space.

In 2004, Voyager 1 crossed the *termination shock*, a region just inside the **heliopause.** At the termination shock, the solar wind decreases suddenly. The craft was able to detect, or sense, this drop. Voyager 1 crossed the termination shock at a distance of about 9 billion miles (15 billion kilometers) from the sun. Voyager 2 crossed the termination shock in 2007, at a distance of about 8 billion miles (13 billion kilometers). In 2013, NASA announced evidence that Voyager 1 had crossed the heliopause, becoming the first craft to leave the solar system.

The need for speed

It took the Voyager craft more than 30 years to reach the edges of the **solar system.** That is an extraordinary length of time for a space mission.

"All things being equal, scientists prefer to work on missions that can be completed in their lifetimes." —Bruce

Bruce Wiegmann became involved in the challenge of travel to the outer solar system through his work at NASA's Marshall Space Flight Center. There, he learned of a unique new form of **propulsion** (pushing a spacecraft) proposed by the Finnish scientist Pekka *Janhunen (yahn HOO nehn).* This form of propulsion is known as the **electric sail.**

Janhunen imagined a spacecraft fanning long wires all around it. When charged with electricity, the wires would act like sails. They would *deflect* (turn away) electrically charged particles in the solar wind, pushing the craft forward.

" Using electric sail technology, we believe we can get to the edge of the solar system in 10 to 12 years. " —Bruce

" If you back up and think about how we get things to the outer solar system, usually it involves launching a traditional chemical rocket from Earth. Once the craft is in space, it fires another rocket to send it on its journey. " —Bruce

Traditional rockets work by burning fuel and other chemicals, called **propellants.**

" Propellants usually account for about 90 percent of the spacecraft's total **mass.** " —Bruce

The electric sail would harness the power of the solar wind, reducing the need for propellants. As a result, the spacecraft would be much lighter. Lighter spacecraft are cheaper to launch. They are also easier to accelerate to great speeds.

In this artist's interpretation, a probe propelled by electric sail technology leaves Earth's orbit.

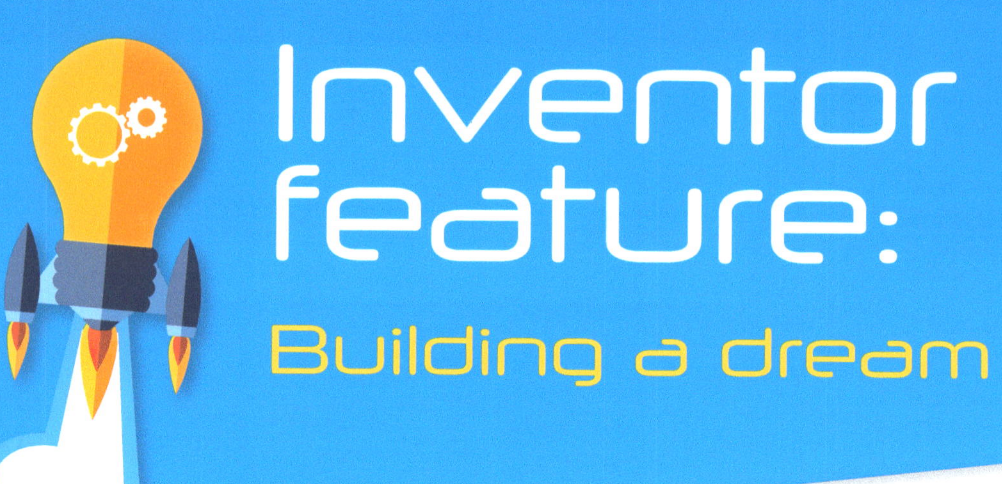

Inventor feature:

Building a dream

The idea of the **electric sail** was developed by Pekka Janhunen, a scientist at the Finnish Meteorological Institute. A director at Marshall Space Flight Center learned of the idea when he met Janhunen at a conference. The director brought the electric sail idea to Wiegmann.

> "We looked at some of Pekka's designs, and, I have to be honest, I kind of laughed at the beginning. I thought there was no way it would work. But after a detailed analysis, my laughter faded, and I said, 'This looks really good.'" —Bruce

Janhunen is a theoretical physicist, a scientist who uses math and reasoning to come up with new ideas about matter and energy. He could demonstrate that the electric sail was based on sound principles. But he could not build the craft himself.

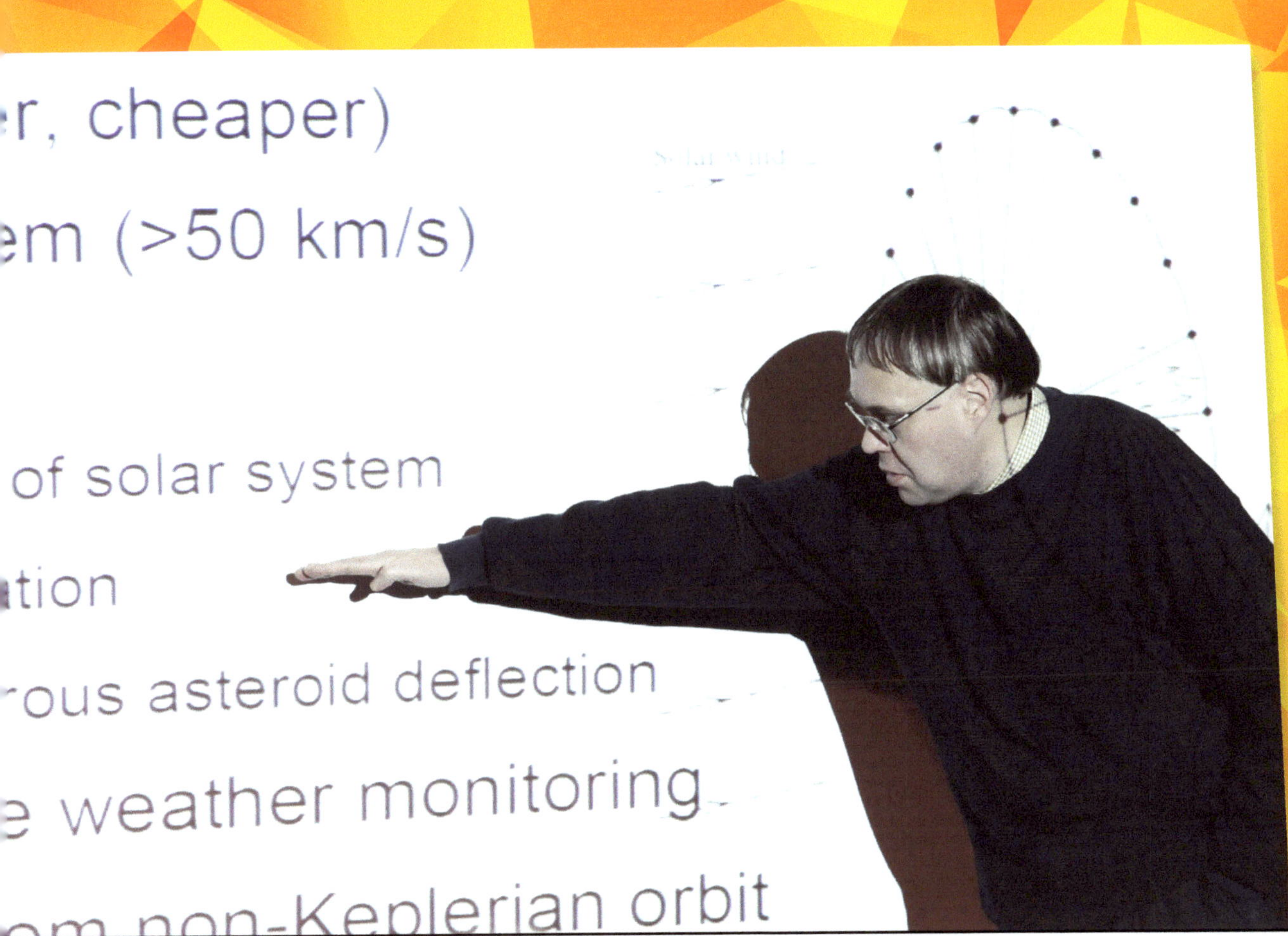

In this photograph, the Finnish scientist Pekka Janhunen lectures about the electric sail concept.

" Pekka's very smart. Sometimes, you see somebody coming up with an idea, and it never gains any traction. " —Bruce

For the electric sail to become a reality, Janhunen would have to work with people who knew how to build it. That was where Wiegmann came in. Wiegmann is a mechanical engineer who specializes in building spacecraft.

Electric repulsion

"Back when I was in grade school, we used to play with little magnets. We called them 'dog and cat' magnets. If the magnets are lined up a certain way, they *repel* [push away] one another. One magnet is pushed away from the other, like a cat running away from a dog." —Bruce

The **electric sail** works according to a similar principle. The solar wind is made up of electrically charged particles. Such particles can have a positive charge or a negative charge. The solar wind is made up largely of two types of particles. There are **protons,** which have a positive charge, and **electrons,** which have a negative charge.

Opposite charges attract, or move toward, each other. For this reason, protons and electrons are attracted. The attraction between protons and electrons helps hold atoms together.

Like charges, on the other hand, repel, or push away from, each other. This causes protons to repel protons and electrons to repel electrons.

" Now imagine you have a long wire floating in space, with the solar wind streaming by. You can electrify the wire, giving it a positive charge. So then you have this screaming proton coming in and approaching the wire. The positively charged wire repels the positively charged proton, in much the same way that magnets can repel each other. "

—Bruce

As the proton is repelled, it pushes against the wire according to the **third law of motion** developed in the 1600's by the English scientist Sir Isaac Newton. That law says that for every action there is an equal and opposite reaction. So, as the wire pushes against the proton, the proton pushes back against it.

Big idea:
An invisible sail

The **electric sail** works because electrifying the wire creates an invisible region of positive charge around it. Any **proton** that enters this region will be *deflected* (turned away). This "force field" around the wire is actually much bigger than the wire itself.

"If the wire is, say, 1⁄25 inch [1 millimeter] in diameter, when you energize it, you get a force field around the wire tens of feet or meters in diameter." —Bruce

This force field is like an invisible tube around the wire. The tube actually changes in size with the amount of charge on the wire. The more charge, the bigger the tube. The tube can be thought of as the "sail" of the craft. So by changing the charge on the wire, you can change the size of the sail.

The bigger the sail, the more protons it deflects, and the greater the **thrust** (moving force) produced. This principle provides a way of steering the craft. Imagine a spacecraft extending charged wires in opposite directions.

Bruce Wiegmann shows the wire thickness that will be needed for the electric sail.

"If one wire is operating at full electric charge, and the other wire is at half charge, the 'sail' will be smaller on the wire with half charge. It will deflect fewer protons, producing less thrust. The other wire will produce more thrust, steering the craft in the opposite direction." —Bruce

Inventor feature:

Basic research

How does an inventor pursue an idea as out of this world as the **electric sail?** For Bruce Wiegmann, the process begins with some basic testing.

" We have a test *chamber* [a roomlike space] at Marshall Space Flight Center. Inside, we have a stainless steel rod that stands in for our wire. The middle part of the rod can be charged to various voltages. Then we fire **protons** at it to measure how they are *deflected* [turned away]. " —Bruce

Wiegmann's test data will be used to develop computer models showing how a full-size electric sail craft would work in space conditions. Such models are being developed with the help of professor Gary Zank, chair of space science at the University of Alabama in Huntsville.

" Dr. Zank has some of the best computer

models of the interstellar medium in the world. He is an international expert. So we are using his talents and his team's talents to help develop our model." —Bruce

The completed model will help to predict the amount of **thrust** produced by different wire arrangements. Wiegmann hopes this will interest spacecraft mission planners in electric sail **propulsion.**

"Spacecraft designed to work in the outer solar system are very expensive, costing billions of dollars. I know mission planners would not want to spend that kind of money on an unproven technology. The models help us to show that the idea could work." —Bruce

Wiegmann's team tests electric sail wire properties in the plasma chamber at the Marshall Space Flight Center.

Protons and electrons

The solar wind consists of both **protons** and **electrons.** So why design the electric sail to *deflect* (turn away) protons, rather than electrons?

" The reason we want to deflect protons is that the **mass** of a proton is so much greater than the mass of an electron. " —Bruce

The **third law of motion** states that every action has an equal and opposite reaction. When the sail deflects a particle, it changes the particle's **momentum** (force of motion). An equal amount of momentum is transferred to the sail.

An object's momentum depends on both its speed and its mass. In the solar wind, both electrons and protons move at great speed. Both are tiny particles. But a proton has about 2,000 times the mass of an electron. So deflecting a proton gives much more momentum to the sail.

But opposite charges attract. So as the wire deflects protons, it attracts electrons.

" Over time, the negatively charged electrons reduce the positive charge on the wire. To prevent that, we must use a device called an *electron gun*. The electron gun draws electrons off the wire and shoots them into space. " —Bruce

This is a representation of how an electric sail might work. The sun emits smaller electrons and larger protons. The probe's wires generate a positively-charged electric field to deflect the protons, which pushes the craft forward. The electrons are attracted to the wires. They are funneled towards the center and shot out into space.

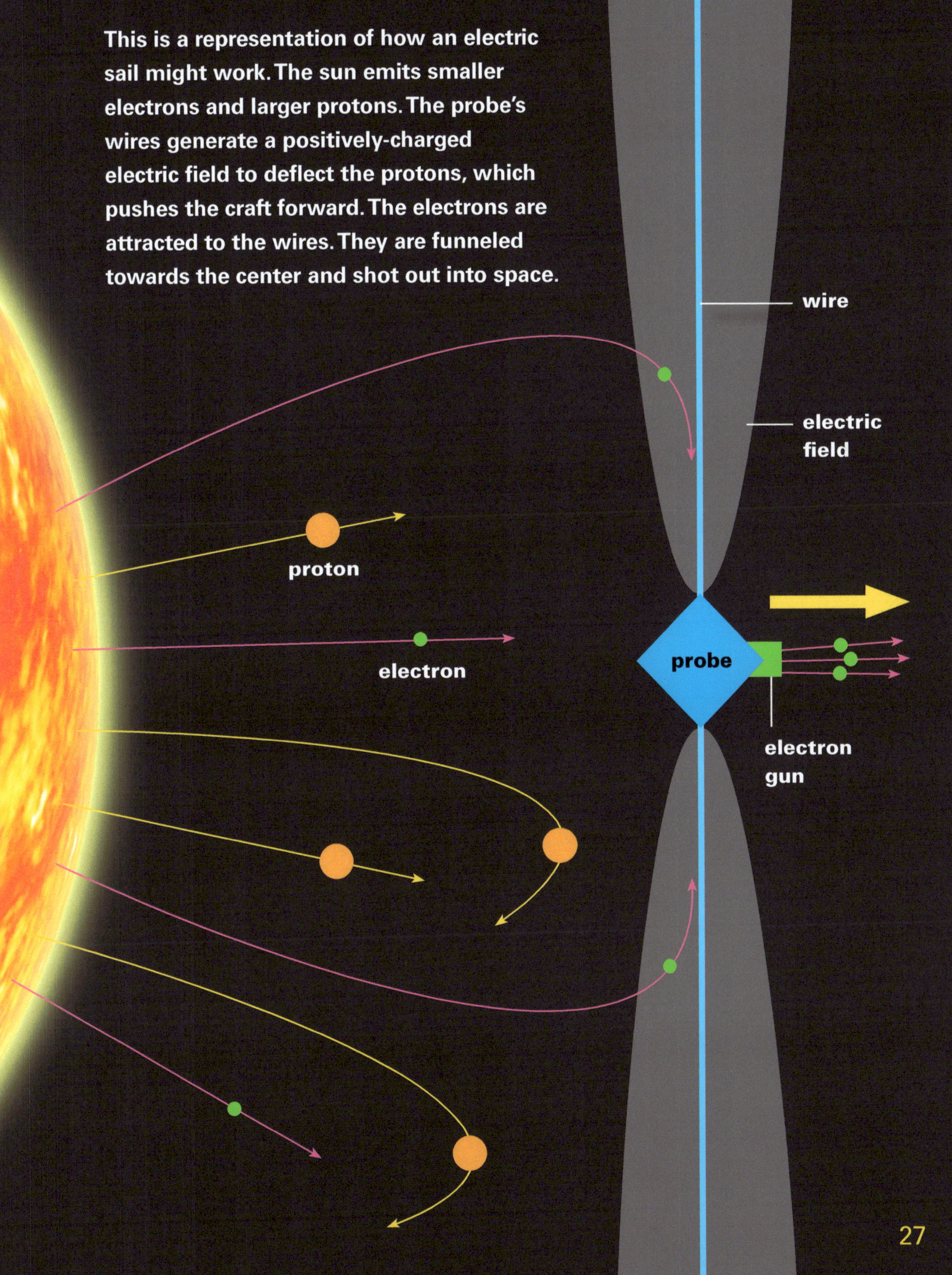

Longer wires

Protons may have more **mass** than **electrons,** but they are still pretty tiny. Each proton *deflected* (turned away) transfers only a tiny amount of **momentum** to the electric sail. To deflect enough protons to propel a spacecraft, the sails must be extremely large. This involves making the wires extremely long. A full-size electric sail craft might require wires extending an astonishing 6 to 12 miles (10 to 20 kilometers) in length.

" To stretch that distance, the wire material will have to be extremely strong. But the material must also be able to carry an electric charge. Some of the materials we are investigating are based on carbon nanotubes or graphene. " —Bruce

Both carbon nanotubes and graphene are *synthetic* (artificially made) forms of the chemical element carbon. Carbon makes up some the toughest substances known, including diamond. Carbon is special because a carbon atom can *bond* (attach) to four other atoms. In a diamond, each carbon atom is bound to four of its neighbors, producing a tough, rigid structure.

Carbon atoms are also bound to several neighbors in carbon nanotubes and graphene. But in nanotubes, the atoms form a microscopic tube shape. The carbon in graphene forms a flat sheet one atom thick. Both forms combine flexibility with some of diamond's legendary toughness.

“ Another key technology is the wire deployer. ” —Bruce

Deploying (spreading out) long, flexible wires in space also presents a challenge. Engineers will have to develop a way to spread the wires out from the craft without breaking, snagging, or tangling them.

“ The United States has not deployed a *tether* [flexible rope] in space longer than 0.6 mile [1 kilometer] since 1996. ” —Bruce

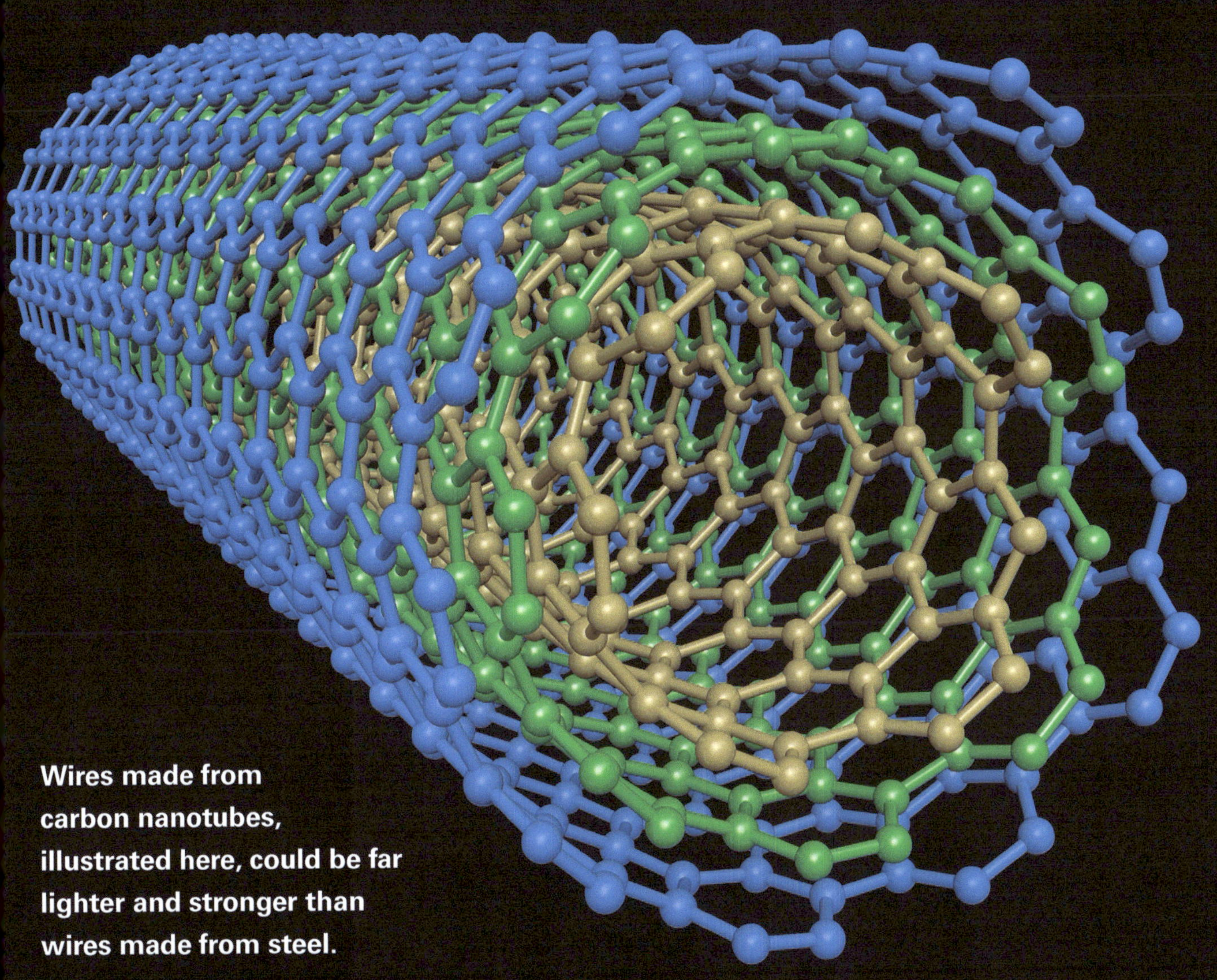

Wires made from carbon nanotubes, illustrated here, could be far lighter and stronger than wires made from steel.

Big idea: Spinning the spacecraft

The total **thrust** produced by an **electric sail** craft is related to the total length of its wires.

" Many people think the best way to get the largest total length is to arrange the craft somewhat like a bicycle wheel. The craft is at the center, and then you have all these wires fanning out like spokes around it. " —Bruce

In such an arrangement, the wires would produce a great amount of thrust. But that presents an additional problem, because the wires are flexible.

" Imagine dipping a tree branch into the flow of a creek or stream. As the water flows over the branch, the branch will bend in the direction the water is flowing. " —Bruce

Likewise, as the **protons** push against the wires, the wires will tend to curl ahead of the craft, pushing them out of alignment. To keep the wires straight, the electric sail craft would rely on a type of movement called **centripetal motion.**

Centripetal motion is movement in a circular path. Have you ever swung a yo-yo or other small weight on the end of a string? The string remains straight, even if the weight is directly above it. This is

because the spinning object has an outward **momentum.** This momentum balances the inward pull of the string, stretching the string tight.

Similarly, spinning the electric sail craft would produce an outward momentum on the wires. This momentum would stretch the wires tight, keeping them from bending.

Artificial gravity. Centripetal motion has also been proposed as a solution to another problem—the lack of gravity in space. Imagine a crewed spacecraft or space station shaped like a giant tube or ring spinning about its center. Centripetal motion could help hold astronauts against the surface of the ring or cylinder, allowing them to walk and work in space more naturally.

Inventor feature:

Inspired by industry

"I grew up in a steel mill town. My mother was a schoolteacher. My father worked in a steel mill." —Bruce

Bruce Wiegmann grew up in West Virginia, in the upper Ohio River Valley region of the eastern United States, during the 1950's and 1960's. Since Wiegmann's youth, many factories and mills have closed in the region. But Wiegmann remembers the area's industrial past.

"At one time in the upper Ohio River Valley, you had Andrew Carnegie in Pittsburgh. You had John D. Rockefeller in Cleveland in the 1800's. You had the General Mills cereal company in Akron, Ohio. The zipper was manufactured in Akron. In 1890's America, Akron was the center of the technology universe, much like Silicon Valley is today." —Bruce

Carnegie was a Scottish-born steel manufacturer. Rockefeller made his fortune in the petroleum industry. As a boy, Wiegmann remembers visiting the region's factories.

" We would go to potteries and watch the workers form clay into bean pots. I was always interested in the mechanical stuff, in the old steam engines, the little copper steam engines that would run the little pulleys. " —Bruce

In this photograph, a very young Bruce is flanked by his mother Forrestine and brother Mark.

Wiegmann was also impressed by the factory workers. Many of them showed great mechanical ability, even though they lacked a formal education.

" Growing up, I remember one gentleman in particular I looked up to. He had only an 8th-grade education. But he was a very, very intelligent man. He worked in the steel mill, and he was a mechanic on the side. He had old mechanic books on aircraft that were built in the 1920's and 1930's. I would go down to his one-car garage, warmed by a wood-burning stove, and we would talk about mechanics for hours. " —Bruce

Wiegmann's interest in machines eventually led him to earn a Ph.D. degree in mechanical engineering. He later went to work for NASA, building spacecraft.

Electric sail vs. solar sail

You may have heard of another kind of out-of-this-world sail craft. It is called the solar sail, and like the **electric sail,** it is powered by the sun.

"The solar sail is a different approach. It reflects *photons.* The solar sail is driven by reflection, rather than repulsion." —Bruce

Photons are tiny particles of light. A solar sail is basically a very large, very thin mirror. Photons from the sun reflect off its shiny surface. As they reflect, the photons transfer **momentum** to the mirror according to the **third law of motion.** In this way, solar sails and electric sails are similar. But the differences are important, especially in the outer **solar system.**

"Sunlight is stronger the closer you get to the sun. As you get farther away, the light spreads out, and the push on a solar sail becomes weaker. Once you get to a distance of 5 astronomical units, it is hard to gather enough sunlight to continue speeding up." —Bruce

One astronomical unit (AU) is equal to the average distance between Earth and the sun. At a distance of about 5 AU lies Jupiter, the largest planet in our solar system.

The particles of the solar wind also spread out with distance from the sun. But as they do, an amazing thing happens to the electric sail. Remember the invisible tube or "sail" of electric influence around the wire? Its size is limited in part by the electric influence of the solar wind itself. As the solar wind spreads out, its electric influence weakens. This actually causes the tube or sail to expand, *deflecting* (turning away) protons from a larger area.

"I like to think of the electric sail craft as a flower, like a daisy. Imagine you have a craft with 20 wires fanning out. Each wire has an invisible sail around it, forming the petals of the daisy. At first the petals are slender, and you have space in between. As the craft moves away from the sun, the petals get wider. The farther you get, the more the petals grow, grow, grow, filling in the space between them." —Bruce

Imagine a solar sail and an electric sail in a race from the sun, and the craft are launched from Earth, at about 1 AU. Which spacecraft would win? The race may be tight to a distance of 5 AU. But at that distance, the solar sail will stop accelerating. The electric sail, on the other hand, will continue to accelerate to about 15 or 16 AU.

Electric sail

Uranus

Neptune

15 AU

20 AU

25 AU

30 AU

Inventor feature:

Other interests

Inventors do not spend all their time in laboratories. They have hobbies and interests, just like other people.

Bruce Wiegmann is a mechanic at heart. He enjoys collecting and working on classic cars.

"I like to go to car shows. I have 8 or 9 cars I am fixing up right now. I have lost count." —Bruce

Wiegmann also enjoys spending time with his two teenage daughters.

"I like cooking. My wife works weekends. So I keep busy cooking and cleaning and shuffling the kids to band and dance rehearsals." —Bruce

Bruce poses with a classic Packard automobile (left). Some of Bruce's classic cars (below).

Left, Bruce with his daughters Victoria (far left) and Lauren (far right) and wife Huiping.

Big idea: Keep it simple!

" Some of Dr. Janhunen's **electric sail** designs have a hundred wires. Some have twenty. At the end of each wire is a small module. Each module is really a tiny spacecraft with *microthrusters* [tiny rockets] to help maneuver the wire. Imagine 20 of these modules connected by long wires to the central spacecraft. That is a pretty complex system. We might be able to do this eventually, but not at first. " —Bruce

To prove that the wires can be deployed correctly, Wiegmann is working to develop a **technology demonstration mission.** Such a mission uses a simplified version of the craft to show that the technology works. The key is to keep the test craft as simple as possible.

" We do not want the mission to fail because we try to use too many wires. If they do not *deploy* [spread out] properly, you could end up with a tangled mess that looks like a bowl of spaghetti. " —Bruce

Instead, Wiegmann envisions a greatly simplified sail craft. This craft would consist of two small modules connected by a single wire.

"Imagine each module is the size of a shoe box." —Bruce

At launch the two craft are right next to each other. The craft would have to get outside Earth's *magnetosphere*, the region shielded from the solar wind by the planet's **magnetic field.**

"The moon is outside the magnetosphere for most of its orbital period. So you just launch a spacecraft toward the neighborhood of the moon, you extend the wires, and you go." —Bruce

Outside the magnetosphere, the craft would separate, spooling out the wire between them to a total length of 10 miles (16 kilometers). Microthrusters on the modules would set the wire spinning end over end, using **centripetal motion** to keep the wire from bending.

"A rate of eight revolutions per day should be enough to hold the wire tight." —Bruce

An *insulator* (material that cannot conduct electric charge) at the wire's center would divide it into two separate sections. Mission managers could vary the charge on each section to steer the craft.

"We just want to prove we can deploy the wires, we can accelerate, and we can steer. Keep it simple. Those three things." —Bruce

Outside the ecliptic

Wiegmann also has a simpler target in mind for the **technology demonstration mission.** Reaching the **heliosphere** would be a long trip for demonstration purposes. But there is a place much nearer to Earth that chemical rockets have trouble going—outside the ecliptic plane.

The matter in the **solar system** is not spread evenly around the sun in all directions. Instead, the planets and many other objects lie within a flat region of space called the ecliptic plane. The ecliptic plane can be thought of as an invisible disk around the sun. Inside that disk are the orbits of the planets and other objects.

The planets and other bodies of our solar system mostly orbit and spin in line with the ecliptic plane. So within the plane, there is plenty of gravitation and **momentum** a spacecraft can harness to help limit its use of **propellants.** Traveling above or below the ecliptic plane is much more difficult and requires more propellants.

Electric sails do not need fuel. They run on the **solar wind,** which blows evenly in every direction. This fact should make an electric sail an ideal candidate for a mission outside the ecliptic plane.

All planets in the solar system orbit in the same ecliptic plane.

"We think we can get an electric sail craft 50 degrees outside of the ecliptic plane within 3 years. That would show that electric sails can do things that chemical rockets cannot." —Bruce

Pushing back the boundaries

" If you look at the automobile industry, Henry Ford developed the Model T, but other people did not have Lamborghinis and Ferraris the next day. " —Bruce

Ford's Model T was the first popular, widely used automobile. Like Wiegmann's **technology demonstration mission** craft, the Model T was designed for simplicity and reliability.

" The first mission out is much like a Model T. You have to make sure it is reliable. You do what you can do. " —Bruce

Wiegmann thinks his craft could be ready for launch by 2021. It is small enough to be launched cheaply, probably hitching a ride with a more expensive mission. It would take three years to get 50 degrees outside of the ecliptic plane.

" If we can prove that the **electric sail** works on a technology demonstration mission, then you can get the scientists on board. Scientists have the need for a **propulsion** system to get a spacecraft where they want it to go. " —Bruce

For scientists interested in the outer solar system, the electric sail would represent a huge advance. A full-size electric sail craft might someday take their spacecraft to the heliopause in 12 years instead of 35, returning the data it gathers within their lifetimes.

The Model T (left) was a simple, affordable automobile. More than 15 million were sold between 1908 and 1927. Below, an artist's conception of an electric sail and how it would work.

Bruce Wiegmann and his team

Members of the Heliopause Electrostatic Rapid Transit System team. Bruce Wiegmann is third from the right.

Glossary

centripetal motion (sehnTRIHP uh tuhl MOH shuhn) a circular motion around a fixed point or axis.

electric sail (il LEHK trikh sayl) a device that uses electrified wires to repel charged particles, producing thrust.

electron (ih LEHK tron) a type of subatomic particle (very small part of an atom) with a negative electric charge.

heliopause (HEE lee oh pawz) the boundary where the solar wind gives way to the interstellar medium.

heliosphere (HEE lee oh sfihr) the region of space around the sun where solar wind is present.

magnetic field (mag NEHT ihk feeld) the invisible region of magnetic influence surrounding a magnet. Earth is a huge magnet with poles called the north magnetic pole and the south magnetic pole. These poles are near, but are different from, the geographic North and South poles.

mass the amount of matter—the stuff that makes up all things—in something.

momentum (moh MEHM tuhm) an object's force of motion. The momentum of a moving object equals its mass (quantity of matter) multiplied by its velocity (speed in a given direction).

quintillion (kwihnTIHL yuhn) a large number that starts with a 1 and is followed by 18 zeros (in the U.S., Canada, and France). A large number followed by 30 zeroes (in Great Britain and Germany). This book uses the definition based on standards from the U.S., Canada, and France.

propellants (pruh PEHL uhntz) fuel and other chemicals used to power a rocket.

propulsion (pruh PUHL shuhn) pushing something, such as a spacecraft.

proton (PROH ton) a type of subatomic particle (very small part of an atom) with a positive electric charge.

solar system (SOH luhr SIHS tuhm) a group of heavenly bodies consisting of a star and the planets and other objects orbiting around it.

technology demonstration mission (tehk NOL uh jee DEHM uhn STRAY shuhn MIHSH uhn) a simplified space mission designed to show that a new technology can work.

third law of motion a principle of physics which says that for every action, there is an equal and opposite reaction; set down by English scientist Sir Isaac Newton (1642-1727).

thrust (thruhst) moving force; a push with force.

For further information

Want to learn more about the sun?

Taylor-Butler. *The Sun.* New True Books: Space. C. Press/F. Watts Trade, Inc., 2014.

Want to perform your own experiments with magnets?

Thomas, Isabel. *Experiments with Magnets.* Read and Experiment. Raintree, 2015.

Want to learn more about Isaac Newton's third law of motion?

Gianopoulos, Andrea. Phil Miller. Charles Barnett III. *Isaac Newton and the Laws of Motion.* Inventions and Discovery. Capstone Press, 2007.

Think like an inventor

Look at these three designs for electric sail spacecraft. For each design, measure the length of each wire in centimeters and add the lengths together. Which design would produce the most thrust?

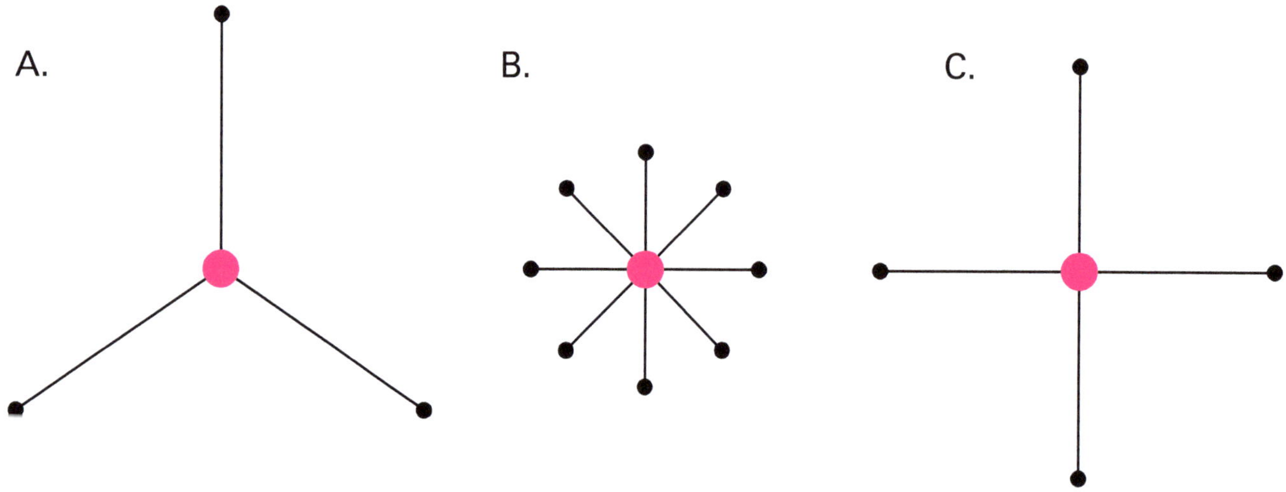

Answer: B

Index

Acknowledgments

Cover	NASA/Marshall Space Flight Center
4-5	NASA/Bill Ingalls
6-7	© Shutterstock
8-9	NASA/Steele Hill
10-11	NASA/Goddard Space Flight Center Conceptual Image Lab
12-13	NASA/SDO/AIA
14-15	© Claus Lunau, Science Source
16-17	NASA/Marshall Space Flight Center
19	Riina Varol (licensed under CC BY-SA 3.0)
20-21	© H.S. Photos/Alamy Images
23	NASA/MSFC/Emmett Given
25	Bruce Wiegmann
26-27	WORLD BOOK illustration by Melanie Bender (© Shutterstock)
28-29	NASA
31	© Shutterstock
33	Bruce Wiegmann
34-35	WORLD BOOK illustration by Melanie Bender (© Shutterstock)
37	Bruce Wiegmann
40-41	© Shutterstock
43	© Bettmann/Getty Images; © Alexandre Szames, Antigravite
44	Bruce Wiegmann
46	WORLD BOOK diagram by Melanie Bender

www.ingramcontent.com/pod-product-compliance
Ingram Content Group UK Ltd.
Pitfield, Milton Keynes, MK11 3LW, UK
UKHW060103300726
14090UKWH00003B/370

* 9 7 8 0 7 1 6 6 6 1 3 8 2 *